THE NATURE OF POOR PERSONS

GIDEON OYIERA OMUDA

ABOUT THE WRITER

GIDEON OYIERA OMUDA IS CURRENTLY A STUDENT AT UNIVERSITY OF NAIROBI UNDER FACULTY OF ARTS TAKING BACHELOR OF ARTS IN COMMUNICATION,POLITICAL SCIENCE AND SOCIOLOGY.HE IS A FORMER STUDENT OF ST.BENEDICT'S BUDALANG'I HIGH SCHOOL,BUSIA COUNTY,KENYA.HIS ORIGINAL HOMELAND IS KANJALA VILLAGE WHERE HE STUDIED HIS PRIMARY EDUCATION IN KANJALA PRIMARY SCHOOL IN BUTULA CONSTITUENCY,BUSIA COUNTY,KENYA.

MR.GIDEON HAD ALSO WRITTEN OTHER WORKS IN HIS NATIONAL LANGUAGE,SWAHILI.HE IS CURRENTLY IN HIS TWENTIES.

MR GIDEON OMUDA CAN BE CONTACTED THROUGH:
EMAIL:womuda@gmail.com
Cell phone:0703654639

ACKNOWLEDGEMENTS

No one writes a book alone.No one publishes a book without the help of many.I want to thank those people here.

In years of my study i met and still meet able and strong individuals called teachers,lecturers,Doctors,Professors and other elites.They made me feel proud of understanding that I own information which am suppossed to deliver.My publishers and other business persons too played and still do play a significant role in my texts.Thank you very much all of you including my fellow students.Credits to your work and am cognisant also to University of Nairobi fraternity.My audience I really appreciate your concern to read this texts.Say hi to my parents at Kanjala village.Thank you too and I,Gideon Oyiera Omuda I do salute you all.Thanks too my friends,are many.

CONTENTS

INTRODUCTION

To my understanding,poverty is ability to lose ones ability and to increase ones willingness,the desire.That means you gain inability.Losing ones ability is an aspect that comes forcefully in the life of an individual though one can as well improve his inability,poverty.Modern days depict poverty as lack of money among the poor people.Some scholars believe poverty lives in a person and other may disagree whether poverty lives with man.I believe that poverty is older than man since man finds his or her inability in an already existing inabilities in society.It is also not clear if people own poverty or whether converse is true because poor people are often heard saying,'leave me with my poverty.'The truth of the matter is that poverty lacks speech instead it has actions.The big question in my mind is that who is supposed to monitor who between poverty and man?In this text you will know how poverty drives the man.

THE POOR AND SOCIETY

A poor is a person who leads life full of inabilities.It may be natural inabilitie if not artificial because some poor persons are born and die poor while others change their status quo.They are the poor persons who hold and accept a big burden,whatever the case,to protect the demands of their rural society.A poor person will always need to live in a rural area.The rural societies you know of are the inhabitants of them.I understand a rural area as a place where the inabilities settle most and well.It is an accommodative point where poverty can be understood well.Poor people are needy due to stability of inabilities in their lives.They tend to settle in place where poverty is understood as a common comfort for the needy.For instance,a poor person who migrates from his or her rural village,going to seek employment in town,will actually live where the nature of his rural village is reflected in that town.For example,take an analogy where a man let me just say a husband from Western Kenya region who moves to seek employment in Nairobi city,he will exactly settle in east area of Nairobi since that is where his inabilities can be well accommodated.He cannot try to live in West of Nairobi such as Westlands because the place does not tolerate inabilities rather,Kibira would be his appropriate concern point to settle.It is for reasons such as nearly free priced foods,easy to pay rentals,poor environmental sanity,which the man from Western Kenya already know exists in Kibera but what the bother.

I assume it true that rural areas make poor people strong and adaptive to harsh environment whatever the cost.Poverty is the best teacher in rural areas and if you asked a poor person who might be his enemy then I expect the answer to be poverty and his poor neighbour.A poor person always identifies himself with another colleague poor.A poor person will always reflect his society since you will learn from him his mode of eating,grooming,speaking and other cultural activities of his or her society.If you want to identify culture of a given society then use its poor.From there you will learn the nature of that culture.Do not use the rich person to determine this since it is difficult to determine the culture of a rich person maybe if he or she was also poor in one point of his life.For that reason poor people always want to compete among themselves in their rural life.And mostly they compete on basis of food;who cook best meals among them,who eats well among them is the question in mind.Sometimes infact more often than note,they may quarrel over the issue.When those from town go back home to their villages,they are the tyranny at home yet the difference is living in different rural areas.When at slums in towns,the poor people tend to look for most energetic requiring jobs to earn wages since they cannot step in office for white collar tasks as the offices cannot accommodate inabilities,they believe.

Ruralites believe to live in rural areas where they can get comfort to drink their cultural liquors and other things related to their culture and that is why you will learn a society's culture from the poor.To illustrate this,if foreign states for example people from US if want to really know the true culture of our country then I would advise them to go for poorest Kenyans.A poor person loves his culture because it is the only wealth he sees in his life.The poorest will tend to protect their lands since it is also important only wealth they own.They then also love to find for those lands among themselves.Other believe too much in their native lands and cannot allow rural urban migration.Land now becomes a special asset of the poor.Poor people love to sell their native land in order to rejoice pleasures of this world.Some love to sell their money to fund their nicy behaviour of drinking traditional liquor.They also love to sell trees in their lands or even exploit their land resources at maximum.They love their society no matter.

Poor love making and maintaining strong social ties among themselves.They love the saying 'unity is strength.'Working and behaving in crowd is their nature.A poor person will blame you if you do not join his or group.For that reason I believe poverty works well in crowd.You will not find a rich man in a crowd of people maybe if he or she wants to gain from the poor people.Watch out and see if that is true.Most of time the poor people believe that it is through group work that they will lead a better life.They do make social ceremonies such as burial,marriage,wedding,small groups,where they can drink,eat,waste their little resources for the sake of social prestige and recognition.A poor person always wants to show of and boast of little he have before the crowd.The worst comes when one owns bigger land than the other;you will know why your land is small under his concern.

The worst comes that the modern poor do not love their fellows.They external show social concern to others when in their hearts they hold a conflicting opinion.I believe that traditional rural poor had open relationship where bads of a person were revealed openly in the eyes of many and story ends there.The modern poor love to hide the bad behaviour they know of their colleagues instead they keep them to gossip from.It true that the today poor understands this and therefore they do not trust each other.When today a poor helps his fellow,he goes to anounce to other group how he saved his fellow.He gossips and when one who was helped notes this,trust loses among the poor since a poor person is an enemy of secret.Especially one who previously was poor and changed his class to better one,loves to boast how he help who in their family,how he will not do it again among other reasons.It is for that reason that today poor people are losing their social bond and individualism will become the order of the day in their societies.But because their love their rural socities,they will come together during occurrence of social issues among them such as deaths.This aspect also makes poor rurals to search for social links with the rich persons.The essence that rich people do not have time to speak about what they have done.A poor person remains to boast of little he had done yesterday.

From the discussion,I do not haste to say that a poor person is the owner of the rural society.They really hate western civilization since it reveals their poor nature.Infact,since being poor occasionally is a forceful element of life,if you want to be in agreement with have nots,do not call them poor.They hate to hear that term and if you are a rich neighbour to a poor person then observe the term since you are at his inspection to whether you know him as the poor chap by mention of the term.Since it is difficult for rich to live together with the poor,rich persons take an initiative to move from their rural lands in search of good homes in town where they buy land,build their homes and live what I know as the running away from the poor.It costs rich to live with poor as we shall see later.It is from that point that I conclude that the poor will remain poor forever since the rich among the poor run away in what I said running away from the poor.Infact the rich person will come back to their native rural land when they need to benefit from the poor people in terms of politics and leadership acquisition.This is why Non-governmental Organizations that help to eradicate poverty will still face the challenge.It is because the few who lead in rural areas are the rich individuals who did practice running away from the poor.After that they also are not willing to help the poor.Rural poor therefore tend to look for social links with rich people who are not close members of their society.For instance,a poor chap from Western Kenya,will tend to look for networks with elites from Nyanza,Central,Kenya and so on.That is why I said that rural societies are owned,maintained and protected by the poor people with regard to the concept of running away from the poor.

In addition,a poor chap is very social,tribal and ethnocentric.One identifies himself with his tribe.Infact a poor person in power is very corrupt,tribal,ethnic centered.Rich chaps do not have time to even thing of their tribe instead they rely on what they have directected poor chaps to do.Infact a rich person does not need his tribe where he works.Poor persons since they defend their cultures,are the one that do practise corruption ones they get a chance.For instance,a poor person is society centered that ones he gets job,he looks where to fix his relatives,family members,tribe members and friends.That is an example of a poor leader.One just believes in helping his society in dubious means to gain social prestige and praise.It is for that reason that I hold that we cannot eradicate corruption without first dealing with the poor.A poor person is not rational in decision making or rather,one is guided by societal needs.Ofcourse I regard the poor as the security guard of culture and traditions.One sees civilization as an enemy of his society.

Despite the fact that they protect their rural social cultures,poor people also tend to organise small committees among them to address the problems that have already occurred.For illustration,thinks of when somebody has died,you find that is their nice time for modern poor to come together,contribute little they have,eat and drink during funeral ceremonies where they also perform cultural activities.It is difficult to see modern poor chaps coming together to prevent a problem they already predict to occur in their very near future insteat they wait,that danger happens and it is when they can come to discuss.For instance,poor people believe when old person is ailing the next obvious think is the ill old will do is to die.In my village in Kanjala,I witnessed many people who can live despite ailing if taken in hospital but they are given chance by my rurals to ail more and eventually die.It is true am a rural,infact an abject poor but I hated the last unity of poor to address a progressed problem.When the sick sick died they all came,cried heavily who killed and contribute their farm products and other things they have.This is the time when their leaders are seen.

Modern poor will lead poorest lives since no great and responsible social ties they hold as their predecessors did in the past.This is because modern poor are many,have poor coordination,resources are scarce and in future I suspect rich people will arise against poor chaps.Rich persons may end up proposing effective ways to do away with poor chaps and the only clear way is effective way to kill them.This is because rich people are increasing in number and they need somewhere to settle.That is why wars will arise and many poor chaps will be the victims.This will form a basis on which to reduce high number of poor chaps in rural areas or slums so as to allow upcoming rich chaps to settle because urban centres are becoming exhaustive.For poor to continue protecting their rural societies they have to make sure they change their status quo.They will not be able to resist the effect of rich people since they will own everything necessary with the ongoing advancing modern world.I believe that rich people hate and do not want to see something like poor person along his or her way.Imagine that is today,what about the future of the poor?Iam sure if rich people will not kill all the poor chaps then the remaining one will be turned to street children and adults to pave space for wealth's settlement.That means poor people will no longer defend their countries since they do not work together,they are weak,and with increased individualism among them that means they will not even know fellow have nots and it will take less than a second for rich people to outdo them.This is becaused developed individuals meet at their work places,have strong discussions and arguments,plans what to do to benefit more and in future they all agree to do away with poor.The only savior if He will come along the way is Sir God and His agents to protect the vulnerable ones.If the God allows Himself not to appear during those times,I hope He would have empowered more some nations that will come in to help the poor chaps.If nothing happens,poor chaps will have no place to exist,produce or just to marry.

I do not understand what will happen in presence of the Lord the creator if He comes to save his poor beings.I really do not understand whether both poor and rich will be given chance to testify before God.I dont understand how the issue will be approached since poor people may cry out why God let them that way as well as rich will do.But I suspect since poor people pray hard to their God,others cry others wail then something good will turn for them in presence of God if He will come.But if He comes,who will be ready to meet that Superior being I here?Will the world turn green,air we breathe change blue or there will be big stones all over?Will water fill the world instead of fire or what?These dangerous animals some of us fear,will they fill and move around freely even meeting myself!What the shit,am not understanding this.Really will those vices we do in our societies secretly revealed?It is just tragedic moment I fill alon my way.Will actually Lord come that way?Ok what I know is that rich people will not outdo poor chaps in presence of God.

From that I think people will have mental,physical and phsychological emotions.From that,is it important for poor to hate rich people and vice versa?If we all want to gain equal favour from God if we all believe in Him we just need to make ourselves equal on earth so that if it means upper class we all help each one attain upper class and so on.I think that is the secret of all of us to attain favour of God,Kingdom of heaven.And I assure you it is possible if all are willing and believe in the God the Creator.But since everyone has his gods on earth then we must have a selected number of people to win the favour of Lord.About God's judgement of us being sinners I dont believe most since all of us are sinners before Him.

Most importantly,the poor chaps really stand for their societies,cultures,norms and even their rural areas.It is difficult to separate a poor from his rural life maybe through education if the poor children are willing to go to school and learn.
Poor believe to be burried in their rural lands.They hold that they want to close to their ancestors.If their deceased succumbed from town,they will

make sure the body is brought back home.A rich one bothers nothing,whether burried or not he or she would have gone.With poor,it is a taboo to burry someone outside his ancestral land.Taboos work well with poor chaps in their societies.They also waste alot on dead bodies than they can waste on live bodies.

Since you cannot isolate themselves from their societies,tribes and ethnic lines,they will continue being poor.Our heroes fought colonialists because they were united.There were no things like tribes and ethnic feelibgs among our heroes.Modern poor persons are very ethnical guided by ethnocentrism and some end up diving themselves into clans,relatives and so on as did colonialists to our heroes who rose up to unity and struggled.Since their is no unity among the poor chaps,poverty is still with them.

Moreover,poor persons like to despise others and themselves.They also believe that nothing good can happen among them and those who struggle to change their status quo are highly discouraged through gossiping,witchcraft and other jealousious activities.Due to this perception among them,rural persons will not easily change their nature of society.They will on cultural values of their societies and ofcourse they will still appear at periphery in their societies.They are conservative and will infact conserve their status quo.

Although rich persons pay alot concern on racism,poor chaps corruption is bound on nepotism,religion and moreso tribalism.People do wonder why tribalism will end in poor societies but what I know is that poverty and tribalism sound like synonyms of each other.Racism is due to prestige while tribalism is as a result of jealous although their end result is hatred that comes with adverse consequences.

THE POOR AND MARRIAGE

Marriage is essential element of the poor.A poor man believes in a polygamous marriage.Since poverty is well with crowdiness,a crowd of wives is crucial to a poor man.Infact one boasts of having many wives.The type of marriage here is come we stay.Marriage is a must for a poor person and if any one alters this is deemed irrelevant in poor societies.Marriage in a poor family is characterised with disagreements among the poor couples.Since illiteracy is the factor,modern poor couples do not understand each other.Divorce and suicide is the order of the day.

There is no discipline in marriage among poor families.Sometimes wives of a poor man tend to disagree more oftenly and jealousy and revenge wins their hearts.They live in desperate situation and in conflictual state of life.Some will obviously practise witchcraft to outdo each other.You will find anomalies in homes of poor chaps among wives,children and man himself.Most importantly they all adapt and lead life of their own.

In addition,marriages in abject poverty are very disorganized.Modern life is very difficult and modern poor women do not like to marry poor men too.They create links with well lived men so as to be sure of good future.In a poor family,aged girl children love boys from wealth families and do start engaging in sexual intercourses at a tender age.Such girls are very weak in mind to the extent that nothing they think of other than their relationships and whether they will be married by wealthy men.Rich men in turn do not also want to marry poor women since they believe nothing important than that in life.Poor girls tend to consult witches to maintain their forcefully befriended rich boys as a result.This type of marriage leads to disorganised relationships.Some poor girls tend to invest in beauty to attract men who are well of but this only ends after sexual intercourse and rich man sends poor girl away.

Poverty has destroyed marriages among poor families.It has made women to become innovative in their lives.Poor women who already are married today love adultery like no body's business.They practise sex outside marriage to earn money,eat and put on well something their poor husbands do not do.Divorce has become the rule of relationship among poor families.Also important,poor couples believe to have a class of children.Children of the poor are many in numbers.They believe among many children there are those who will bring luck in their families.A poor father will advice his sons and daughters to marry wisely,that means to look for well off girls and boys.They search to change the status quo whatever means.It is from that that a poor is identified through his number of wives and husbands in conjunction with number of his children and divorce undertaken.

Marriage in poor family lacks rationale.Poor chap believes that the importance of marriage is sexual intercourse.When marrying,a poor chap considers no other factor in life.A poor girl is not after the behaviour of one to marry instead money is the issue.Poor boys do not actually love for the sake of it.They just marry to make society happy,have children and enjoy frequent sexual practices.Girls do the same.There is no plan for marriage among the modern poor.Handsomeness,beautifuliness and money if not wealth are the basis point of modern poor fellows.No other considerations at all.As lives become difficulty in marriage and sexual practice bores,relationships reache to a halt among poor moderns.Stressful life wins their emotions and suicide becomes the gate to their homes.Poor chaps love to kill themselves,are vulnerable to die in their own hands.

Girls and boys from poor families do like relationships at a tender age.Especially those from 12 to 20s already are not virgins.Poor chaps like boy girl relationships.To some extent,others are forced to marry among themselves when early pregnancies find their tender relations.This forced marriage help poor become more poor.This is also important feature of the modern poor.You can consult among yourselves and find how marriage found your friends.

With many children in poor families,children face difficults and since thet have no option to divorce,some adapt and become innovative chaps.Children in poor families become small thieves at home.They start from stealing eggs,hens upto extent of turning out as special thieves and goons.Such children do run away from their homes to where they do not know.Some become street children and adults,others join gangs to invest in theft.That is why it will take long for governments in developing countries to eradicate theft before addressing the issue of poverty.

Marriage is a routinal activity in lives of the have nots.Modern poor have no respect marriage.For instance a girl goes in the house of a boy and stacks their claiming she wants to marry the boy especially if the latter is from wealthy family.A poor chap follows no legal procedures to marry since law is viewed as expensive route to reach to their destinations.With poor,laws of state are deemed more expensive than other expensive things they know.

Since poverty is an enemy of marriage,poor persons involve in hopeful ideologies in their lives which help their wives tolerate their poor men.Women adapt and become strong instruments of work in poor families.Children are also taught the importance of working hard in those homes.Women in poor family lives comparing her husband with others.Even those women who are in deep marriage declare that they love their poor husbands.Also important is that a woman of a poor man must give in to other fellows.A poor man is very polygomous.Children are many in number in underdeveloped persons since sexual intercourse lacks organization,belief that children are wealth and so on.Such believes make homes of poor persons being filled by many children of the same sizes,others with abnormalities and so on.In those homes when you step in,environmental pollution by children through defaecating,sounds,poor clothing and malnutrition related diseases are the order of the day.It is a pathetic life for both children and women.This forces men to commit suicide or just die at younger age since they can not meet all demands in their poor homes.Ofcourse most of underdeveloped homes are led by poor widows who lost their husbands.

Furthermore,there is no faithfulliness in marriage among the modern poor as did the old chaps.Infact the extent of poor persons' marriage is reaching a degree where a woman wants to behave like her husband,having more husbands than usual.That is the nature of marriage among the poor.Their relationships are of shamefully deeds.

Modern poor girls love relationships and sometimes do practise temporary marriages.For them,marriage does not serve any other important role but a road map to look where one can settle her problems.This is because in poor families girl children persevere to stay with their parents and when trouble persists is when they run away from their homes to look for a must boy to marry.Such girls are very easy nut to crack and tend to have low say in marriage.Their husbands despise them and their marriage ends up a field of problems,no peace no respect.

Another important feature of poor children is that they love to stay with their well of relatives.That is why in most cases you will hear marginalised children say that they stay with their uncles,ants,sisters and so on.This may work well with poor girls and not boys.It is because girls do almost all chores at home like maid work,cleaning,cooking among others.The boys do not work well since a poor boy is very rude.A poor boy has experienced difficulties in his poor life and therefore his head can be compared to a stone.Most of time you will learn that poor children do not respect their parents and more often such parents hold the children's heads are very hard and they end up sharing insults whether children inherited rudeness from their mothers and mothers sides or fathers'.This creates disunity among modern marriages.

Another important element of modern poor is that children are highly separated from their parents.Parents care less about their children who seek some comfort to relatives and other children for instance boys can move to search for small jobs like herding and do on.If they do not succeed they turn up to make good street children and adults.Girls tend to look for cleaningness jobs,maid among others.

Modern poor chaps who stay in slums in towns today invests in good mode of grooming.They want to put on well for the case of youths to attract their opposite sexes.Old poor in slums do careless and put on their rags.The poor fellows in rural areas are rag owners.You can identify a poor chap by the way one puts own and how clothes shape his or her body as we shall see in the next topics.

Marriage in poor families is characterised with bottle necks because of actions of poor fellows who own little resources than their fellows.Such comrades do attract married girls with some resources so as to engage them in sexual matters.Their tricks succeed and this renders problems in poor families.Such comrades among modern poor sicieties are the one who spreads sexually transmitted diseases,Hiv and Aids among poor families.In addition,married girls more oftenly conceive babies who do not belong to their actual husbands.This is the nature of poor persons' marriage.A modern poor man does not respect wives of his fellow men instead he looks at them as potential partners especially if they are beauitiful.

In modern poor socities,marriages occur between young girls and boys.And if went to nearby hospitals you will find very young girls carrying their own babies.Their husbands tend to look old at their tender age because they struggle to meet the needs of their young families.In many occasions parents of these young couples are one left with burden to take care of those young families.

Following those reasons,poor male persons in modern societies fear to marry even when their age is much enough since they need first to change their status before they can marry.Marriage is only good for successful people in poor modern societies though poor persons marry to fulfil societal dreams.Since it is not easy for poor people to be renamed wealthy and rich in their lives,poor girls will suffer to get husbands and thus contemporary poor persons will experience women living alone as well as men.And where they mary in faith of society and religion,life still becomes difficult in their marriages which results to divorce.Marrige is now optional among poor families.It is only poor young children who take life easy and marry without having knowledge of the world view among poor societies,persons and rural areas and that is why you will find young girls in poor societies either pregnant,have their families and their husbands in their tender age.It is that pathetic and in most cases they contract very contagious diseases and that is why among poor families people dies at youth stage.That is how poverty makes marriage irrelevant in modern poor societies.

As much as governments are struggling to fight dangerous diseases and other issues,it will be difficult to make it without dealing thoroughly with poverty among their citizens.Poverty is the root cause of all problems of this world we live in and any person who will really want that our world become a better place to live,one must change the status of poor persons to happier stage or one who will really fight for social equality and classless society with is just a mere dream.Iam sure of one somebody who can do that,only God either by Himself or if He soothens the hearts and minds of rich persons to embrace equality.The problem is poor persons really need to become either rich or semi-rich but in contrast,rich people do not want to test semi-rich nor near poor life instead they need to be more and more richer than their normal state.Since they both use same resources on earth,that is poor and rich and the rich persons are the controller and owner of those resources,they will not allow poor persons to use their resources fully to change status quo.That is why rich people are very selfish.Poor ones are not such selfish as compared to their commanders because they need to join,form groups where they can help themselves in unity.But as they form such groups,if their members have last to test richness,they cause havock in those groups.For that reason,even unity among poor societies is a big problem.If you want unity chase poverty.

Poor persons also tend to marry within theirs tribes among poor societies.The only far place a poor person can marry is in or from a very close neighbouring society.This affects unity in poor societies and lack of peace becomes a factor.

That explains why poverty is an enemy of marriage and in that case where poor persons marry,religion becomes a bonding force in terms of faith for poor couples to live well.But when religion or church values become irrelevant among poor couples with time,their marriage dissociates.As much as poor girls in modern societies think of marrying rich persons,it is difficult since a rich person does not tolerate poor persons,when they are exploited,they become useless.It is true no rich man wants to marry poor persons unless on contract for sexual malpractices and if rich persons have some abnormalities or dangerous disorders that they want to infect beautiful poor chaps and move on.It is such truth that a poor person in modern society cannot change her status through marriage.That is why we have many unmarried women in modern poor societies.The other issue of concern comes where modern persons especially girls put on sexy attires to track rich men for marriages.There mode of grooming to be tue,can only attract contract for payable sexual intercourse and not marriage.A rich man will only marry a rich woman.It is troublesome for poor chaps since a poor woman is not willing to marry a poor man in modern poor societies.It is the reason why marriage among poor persons is not stable.

THE POOR AND ECONOMY
Most of economic activities spend a lot and earn little for the poor.The main economy activity of the poor people is agriculture.You can imagine how poor chaps cultivate their lands manually,waste their energy,spend a lot on their farms and earn little from agriculture.Think of a farmer who sells one banana at five shillings.That poor chap is one who need to buy infact a mobile phone that was made in less than an hour by rich industrialised persons at five thousand shillings.How many bananas will the poor chaps produce and sell in order to buy that phone?Iam not a good mathematician but I suspect the farmer will improve his bananas five hundred times.Then guess what,how long will it take for a farmer's farm to produce those five thousand bananas?Then from their tell me if

over reliance on agriculture will help change the status quo of the poor persons.

I believe that industries can help change this if agriculture is not advanced through technology.A poor chap will toil and moil in his or her farm for several days I suspect in vain.Just hold on,if we rely on agriculture we poor people,population is increasing will we actually in future find somewhere to cultivate?Agriculture today requores a lot of capital to practise but a poor person is totally broke.My poor grand father passed away cursing the world by its wonders.He cultivated the land for long yet he died a very poor chap.He became old,many wives(my grandmothers),no energy to cultivate,bend back and walking in support of a stick.

In poor societies very early in the morning poor chaps carry jembes on their backs,dressed in rags,their waists tied with pieces of dirty clothes,children are woken up to go to shambas forcefully and other children who refuse to dig are beaten thoroughly and even denied food.Poor parents advice their children to invest in farm,cultivation.Ofcourse they urge children to work hard in shambas since it is backbone of their lives.I tell if you are rich person try visiting a poor family early in the morning,you will see marvellous.I do not want to mention looming grass thatched houses,children where they sleep,it is very awkward state and imagine on the previous night they slept hungry.They just adapt.The hope of a poor chap is shamba and that is why poor chaps have conflicts over land ownership.They kill each other in either way to acquire lands.Poor families are always in constant struggles over their lands.Disagreements over land among poor countries will continue since their population increases day in day out.No land to live,to farm,and graze among modern poor chaps better the earlier group of poor.Since they rely on agriculture their economic status will not change.They will lack where to cultivate and therefore may also end up working on the farms of the richmen.

To curb conflicts among the poor,I think governments in underdeveloped countries need to introduce the culture of industries where poor people can work.A poor farmer cannot compare himself with somebody who earns a salary(ies) per month.Rich people will maintain their status because they have knowkedge if industries.I assure you no one agriculturalist i mean can outdo an industrialist.No no forever.A farm will produce his cheap agricultural products,give them to an industrialist in form of raw materials who will in turn sell to poor chap finished goods at a very high price.Guess what,a poor farmer taking several month to produce items from farms to sell at a very cheap price while a richman in turn sells motorvehicles manufactured in less than a week to make millions of money per vehicle.I do not see bright future with a griculture as the main economic activity among the poor chaps.

Agriculture for a poor society to change it must be used as a minor economic activities.Poor chaps also tend to practise small business like activities like that I mentioned of selling very cheap items.Business can do well for a poor chap if he will improve on modes of items to sell.You cannot sell bananas and you claim to be rich.State in poor societies need to facilitate enabling business activities.The problem here is that poor chaps lack enough capital to start business,lack knowledge to keep business records among other obvious things.It is responsibility for a state to support these marginalised groups through funding and education.

Modern poor men are lazy and most of work is done by women in pure societies.Men waste their time chatting along the transport networks and thus contribute alot to poverty status in their lives.In poor societies women work hard than men although the winingful nature of gender equality today favours women and thus men are forced to work in pure families and where necessary beaten up by their wives.Such men waste most of their time drinking alcohol from morning,get drunk and make alot of noise to their families tending to know more than others in this world.Children learn this and as a result start taking illicit brews at a tender age.That is why NACADA will take long to achieve its ambitions to eradicate drug abuse in presence of poverty in Kenya.Infact government exists to deal with poor people.To help control and assist them in their life.A state that has no concern to its poor then plants poverty.If the state continues to serve its rich men then the state of developmet in those countries is underdeveloment.They are these poor people among us that group a country into a third world category.The state needs to help transform the lives of poor people if it means to serve and this is achieved when poor chaps support their governments.

It is true that parents in poor societies advice their children to marry strong couples who know to cultivate.Some modern poor need their sons and daugthters to marry educated in-laws.They really want change in their lives.Modern men are deemed lazy because they do not work instead they stand along the streets make noises,eat in local hotels and go back to their homes.Infact most of modern poor men are very idle.I think they do not want to work in farms anymore.Thirld world countries need to invest in such people through industries where poor men can work.Developed governments do not exploit its poor citizens through agriculture instead they develop through industries.

Another economic activity of the poor people is visiting relatives and maintaining strong ties.They travel to see their relatives in search for help in form of food and money albeit,modern poor are very individualistic and they do not want such visitors.You will hear poor families rely on their unlaws for survival.Also important is that poor parents take marriages of their children as a business point to get wealth.This is through dowry and other marriage payments.This is because such parents view dowry as a final salary of their hard work and in most cases those poor chaps set high bride price for their daughters' marriage a factor that leaves their husbands mesmerised.Inlaws to a poor family face alot of challenges because of overdependence.Seeking for help is their economic activity.

Furthermore,organizing marriage ceremonies is another economic activities of the poor people.Poor families tend to invite their inlaws for functions where they set to gain.In such occasions you will hear a lot of prices set for greeting elders,washing hands to eat,and many others especially if inlaws are well off.They waste alot in eating food during such ceremonies.Infact poor people believe that relationship is in stomach.So they tend to spent a lot on food.You can identify the poor through hospitality.

Borrowing is another economic activity for the poor people.You cannot sepate poor chaps from borrowing.One can borrow food from friends,money,and many other things.The problem arises when to repay.A poor person is not prepared to pay back and as a result you can quarrel over repayment.Modern poor persons now borrow money from banks,when they fail to pay banks do impose serious revenge on them.A poor men hate banks since they know banks do exploit them very much.Some curse why banks are mecessary evil.Infact most of poor chaps do not have bank accounts.What they fear is high interests associated with banks if you borrow from them and low interests accrued to some elite poor when they save in banks among poor societies.Infact if the governments need to know current problems in their countries,let them consult from the poor persons.A rich person may need feel the effect as poor one does feel.

Religion has become industries of poor chaps.Iam not telling poor persons to stop serving God but between God and poor people who is rich?Poor people do waste most of their times going to churches and most of them do nothing since they actually do not mean to serve their God.What they do is to pay little amount of things they have to wise poor chaps who want to benefit from them in the name of God

Gossiping is another job of a poor person.They love gossiping the progress of people.A poor person gossips thoroughly.Poor childrens gossip like no body's business.The only place they can meet and agree is when they have something their can gossip of.Remember all these activities earn them nothing.There are no items or money someone can earn through gossiping and what have you.This is accompanied by telling stories,listening to music and so on.

Theft is also an important practise of poor people.You can identify a poor persons through stealing.Poor children start by steal things at their homes until they turn up to big thieves.They force to still since poor thieves believe in force as we shall see later.They are energetic and some may do eat alot,do practices to become big bodied so as to fear and still from their clients.This is why as poor people even when employed they have a culture of stealing in their jobs.They become corrupt and actually destabilise the activities of state.Corruption is a form of theft and if not,the two work hand in hand with each other.Corruption is rampant in Kenya because we have some poor chaps who want to steal from people.When the idea is shared among the peripherals i.e poor and the cores i.e rich,the core outdoes the poor since he owns everything.For that reason,corruption is directly linked to poor persons and to eradicate corruption,let poverty be addressed fast and first.

Witchcraft is another source of the poor persons.A poor person when in difficulty or just in jealousy state,one tends to consult magic and others own the magic power.A poor is not an agent of laws and is not willing to undertake judicial procedures.To him following legal procedure is long process and waste of time or rather,one takes law in his hands and deal with the matter alone if difficult they meet in witchraft arena.That is why you will see poor persons prefer mob practices.They will continue maintaining their social status since witchraft is a destroyer to development of any individual.Poor person believe in magic and if they get employed they steal sick the support of their magics.They believe that witchraft is good judge to punish their enemies and achieve everything they want.In the long run their families inherit abject poverty.That is why you will hear poor people saying that can witch one to get or not get job,if they want to marry they go to their witchdoctors,if if employed and need promotion they use witches as so on.Some creative poor do see witchcraft and allege the practice wisely to wit their clients they know everything instead money is the factor.Witchcraft is an enemy of development and witchdoctors themselves are very poor.Some modern witch are said to have gone to school abit and they use their little knowledge to claim they are followers of God,i.e prophets instead they need to benefit from the people.In poor societies it is difficult to realise who is really the servant of God.That is why I do not trust the salvation of poor persons.Through witches,poor persons on dubious extraordinary things inform of beings which they they believe to be their masters and judge.They use their magic to get wealth and to protect them against their enemies.Their have their gods who they believe to be everything on this earth.As much as poor people claim to be holy and christian or any other religion,their faith is questionable.And it is true because in poor societies poor people do not trust salvation of others since they know what they do in contrary.

Making relationships.Another economic activity of poor people is to create links with elites where they can get support from.Poor girls and boys love boy girl relationships especially girls who want to get support for their survival.In most cases among poor societies girls and boys love to always together and as a result waste most of their time in unproductive relationships.As modern poor girls look for relationships to get money,other support in life and to enjoy,modern poor boys are in need of sexual intercourses alone and move on.Poor girls as a result suffer a lot in relationships like those especially where they thought to be a nice place to settle their problems.Modern poor boys do the act because they fear expenses associated in those relationships which thet cannot afford.As a result poor girls today tend to ignore poor boys and go for those in well off families who in turn do not like poor status and in that case,relationships in modern societies do not favour poor persons.As a result,girls from poor families may turn up to become commercial sex workers since their marriages either did not do well or lack future and unpredictable.This makes especially poor girls lead stressful lives more than boys since rich persons are one are safe in modern world.Through this children of poor persons will suffer a lot.The only solution to poor families in that case is through education.Those who do not attain education to maximum will be the victims.That is why governments in developing countries cannot eradicate prostitution without addressing poverty in their regions.Also important is that modern poor girls have realised that richmen want beautiful ladies and therefore they struggle a lot to become beauitiful to attract men of their choice.Poor men relies on residue of girls that have been used by richmen and dumped since they have no option.That is why you will never find a virgin poor aged girl until they learn from here or elsewhere and change.Poor boys face difficulties to find beauitiful girls in presence of rich men because they lack resources to maintain them yet they have desire to have beauitiful partners.As a result poor boys theoretically engage in sexual relations with beauitiful ladies they admire through masturbation activities.This makes such poor boys and men to become rapists of they do not thing of raping girls.Disadvantaged poor girls end up using some material assets to accomplish their sexual desires.Some very poor girls who cannot afford such material things use items like bananas to virtually enjoy sex with boys they admire in mind.Relationships among poor persons is not stable and disorganised.But because of their problems,very poor persons tend to think of faithful relations but since faith without actions(resources to facilitate) is dead,relationships among poor societies face alot of challenges.Girls find favour to get jobs and if such girls get jobs they make work place bedrooms of their behaviour.That is the nature of pure people.

Unemployment is the employment of poor persons.Poor persons tend to be idly.Idleness among the poor people think criminaly in their undertakings.The only answer a poor person knows when you ask one why idling is that there are no jobs.Most of them are poor men.The truth is that sending them to cultivate land will not make them solve their immediate problems.What can help them is industries which are not enough to accomodate them and in many cases in their rural societies their are no industries.Such men tend to rely on help if political leaders in their centres of idleness where they discuss a lot of issues from dawn to dusk.Political leaders give them some money inform of lunch and drinks.They get home and found no food since their wives go to shambas to cultivate for future needs.This brings chaos in poor families and breakages of marriage.As a result some poor men move to urban centres to stay in slums where industries can make them place to work and in some cases no jobs in industries and thus become hustlers who do any jobs available in urban centres.Those small jobs in urban centres earns them little instead food.In urban areas there exists issue of rents and remember problems in their rural areas.This makes such men sleep outside streets if they cannot secure old iron sheeted,grassed,mad and paper bagged houses that are relatively cheap.Such men get their meals of their days were successful from local hotels and eat just not to feel hungry.Their wives in rural area remain the beast of burden since their husbands make no move in slums of urban centres.Some men do not get back home until their deaths to extent that ruralites contribute money and resources to facilitate their burials.Those who survive turns to street adult depending on how and when did you are in the urban centres.Others go back home very old and find their wives bore children not of their own and others find their wives already have husbands.It is that pathetic situation among the poor people.Others their wives follow them in towns where they face the challenge and become prostitutes in urban centres to cater for their lives and some for their children.That is what poverty means.

Pastoralism either pure or semi serves as another main source of income among poor families.It will be difficult for poor pastoralists to grow.Some keep large and small number of livestock which helps pay marriage price.In that case,in modern poor societies with increased population,their is no enough land to support large herds of cattle.This means that land is not available for pastoral poor persons.Due to this reason,poor pastoralists tend to engage in wars and conflicts for land tenure among poor pastoralists societies.That is where criminality starts as raids using the concept of gun culture are conducted.Life for poor chaps is very pathetic.Women exploitation is rampant among poor societies but since modern societies defend gender equality without social equality,conflicts will order the days among such poor societies.There is need to face poverty first than to start with any other issues since poverty is the root cause.

Aids and especially grants.Dependency on aids is another economic activity of a poor person.Such persons do get food from donors,and other stuffs to help them live.A poor person lives hoping that one day through lack he will get a donor to give them grants to change their status.Modern poor persons do borrow money from banks.The money they get is not used effectively and therefore becomes difficult for them to repay and highest interests associated with banks in modern poor societies.As a result,poor persons lands are taken by banks to repay those loans including other material things that poor persons own.This encourages poverty among poor societies.No one can become a better person through such a scenario.That is why economy of poor persons is weak.Poor persons are used by rich persons to become poorer as wealthy becomes richers.Since poor persons want also to feel well to handle wealthy and in this case inform of loans,they will not change their status since it will become difficult for them to repay instead,they will lose all they have to repay and interest.In modern poor societies poor persons go for loans.Morally,poor minds are weak,want also to become rich and if banks entice them with some good hopes of becoming rich through loans,poor persons end up getting urge to go for loans.My advice there is that a poor person cannot change through high interesting loans and long procedures of getting those loans.If governments in poor societies want their economy to grow,then their bank interests should be low as much as possible as in rich societies.

Innovations.Modern poor people are becoming innovative to help them enhance social mobility from their original social class.These are those educated poor persons.Some try their luck in technology,games,talents.This has also led to commercialization of churches and other religions.Today poor persons use media to earn for their life.They have become more creative a lot that other illiterate poor are used to make them rich.This will in turn lead to social conflicts when the exploited poor realise that other literate poor persons want to grow through them in dubious means.We have seen talents doing well and poor persons will therefore invent more talents to earn.Modern poor persons are in a struggle of becoming rich but where they misuse,mislead and mistreat their fellows,conflicts will occur when the exploited realises.I love use of talents as a good way to change social status.I do not like self centered poor persons who use technology in bad ways to ruin others for instance,one opens a company online,names it and tells poor persons to join in many large numbers after paying subscription fee,and you earn as you introduce new members.Such scrupulous business persons organise fake interviews where poor persons pay for the interviews which bears no good resilts.Those are examples of innovative malpractices taking place in the poor societies among the poor persons.You find that poor persons waste their time and their other little resources to try secure such fake employment opportunities.They will not change their status if they use such methods since such companies produces no goods to export or just use to sustain their life.Poor innovations among modern poor is another form of exploitation among poor societies.

Interestingly,modern poor persons believe that money is not everything.Those who maintain the notion are very and absolutely poor albeit others have learnt to disregard the pretex due to severe modern economic demands.

THE POOR AND COMMUNICATION

You can determine a poor person through his or her communication.This is through facial structure,body shape,types of clothes one puts on and to a more extent vernacular speaking.

A poor person throws words without any prior considerations.They claim to be best speakers yet one speaks from unsound mind.A poor person is not concerned with type of language to use or type of context.Their communication is poor.Infact their communication is good as in gossiping,making noise and insulting.Meet a poor woman in a wrong corner and see how she will spit venom on you.Mouth to a poor person is another weapon.It does not serve his communication role but security role.A poor persons speech do lack logical sequence of ideas and organization.

A poor person is bitter and always believes to war as the only solution.A poor person is bitter and jealous of rich people and in most cases,you will hear communication or just speeches of poor persons attacking the rich or praise the rich persons to gain favour from rich individuals.You can detect anger or pleasing aspect in the communication of poor persons towards rich people.In modern poor societies poor persons use words of mouth to lament or please rich persons.Since poor persons fear being victimization from rich persons,even when given chance to speak they do not say the truth.A poor person will only say truth in crowds and not when a lone because they fear outcomes of their truthfulness by the core ones.In modern poor societies the communication of poor persons is not theoretically based but a throw of any information in the mind of a poor chap.One can detect corruption through communication of a poor person in poor societies.Corruption is poor societies is class based since those in upper class favour themselves as well as those in lower social class but theirs is not such beneficial.

Poor persons do not own any means of communication in poor societies and media is owned by those in the top class.Such media exists to serve the owners and rich persons.Since modern poor are keen on their status of life due to difficulties and enabled inabilities in their lives,they are bitter,speak harshly about the rich people.Infact since poor persons believe in fighting,tends to reach revolution as the only way to finish up those at their top.I am sure it is difficult for poor persons to war against rich persons in modern societies.The rulers in the poor societies are the rich persons,own everything coersive,technology including communication and in such cases modern poor persons cannot attempt to war rich persons unless if rich persons fight among themselves.Their difficulties in life make poor persons communications to be rough.

Since they are based on ethnocentric lines,poor persons will always want to speak in their vernaculars.Poor persons speech portrays accent of their mothertongues.Poor people will always speak noisily in their mothertongues and if you judge them against that fighting is their concern.A poor person is determined through quarrelsome activities and conflictual nature.A poor person is anarchical and very bitter since one survuves through dangerous diseases,harsh environment and other difficulties of life.Poor persons are bitter such that death is their only vision,either kill or be killed.They are very rude and communication of a poor person depicts rudeness in him.An empty debe makes loud noise the same is the fearure of the poor persons.Because of their bitter and jealousious feelings,poor persons tend to fight in their families and conflicts and war is their language.That is why when dealing with poor persons one has to be keen,because a small issue results to war and the worst comes when they are in crowds,mob activity is for poor people I mean.In mob is where poor persons can fully shore their conflictual nature,they can steal,fight,kill in mob.

Even as Tv and radio presenters are always happy to report their news,poor persons are bitter with them.Some even do not listen.It is because they are hungry and they cannot tolerate your presents.They are jealous to extent in which they ask how newsreporters got that job,why they did not become journalists.The worst comes when news do not favour poor persons,they wail in bitterness wherever they are.That is how poverty affects communications and reason why media is supposed to fight for eradication of poverty.Since media among poor societies are profit oriented and do alot of commerce than service to the poor persons,poverty still will continue since modern media fetches the little poor have in modern societies instead of helping change their status.The communication in modern poor societies has become an expensive commodity for poor persons.Because poor person lack adequate information in modern societies because of illiteracy as a matter of poverty,they still have long way to go.When poor persons see rich persons in good clothes,driving good vehicles,having best modern communication tools,the bitter they become.Some learn from their bitterness to become thieves and others good complainers.

When rich persons speak language not of their own societies,poor person are not happy about it.They just think bad about it.For example in my country Kenya a rich person speaking in English really hurts the hearts of poor Kenyans.Poor persons believe in language of their own.When you do that,poor persons assume you despise them because they did not have privilege to go to school.In that case they can employ their form of punishment.

The communication of a poor person shows the need for good governments in poor societies to help eradicate poverty through helping the poor.Education in modern poor societies should not be only solution since a poor person cannot learn well and if he does,one cannot eat knowledge unless through knowledge and that is after someone has been employed.It is in modern poor societies where people have put all value of life on education alone.Am a staunch supporter of education but I do not believe much in kind of education offered in poor societies to be a solution to poverty.Infact the modern poor persons are/wii be educated people as we shall see later on.

A poor person is very bitter and fierce being.Poor persons are like animals that hunt others for food,shelter and mate.A poor person is very troubled compared to animals since some live in game parks,others are treated fairly good for example dogs for rich persons.You can imagine of any dangerous wild animal,she is better of than poor persons.The people of

very low class in poor societies you cannot trust them,infact when you are rich person handling poor persons is dangerous,those people are bitter and are thinking of killing,you do not actually know what a poor person is thinking for you if you are better of.One just need to be keen when handling poor person.The worse comes when they are in group(s),peace and cooperation becomes silent terms.It requires God ardor to deal with poor persons.They are very anarchical whether children or adults.Such behaviours make poor persons become criminals in poor societies.You will find poor children are thieves,murderers in poor societies as well as poor adults.In urban centres they live in slums where youths steal,have rude kind of communication without good mannerism and etiquette.Poor adults employ the same language as those youths and in towns they make security a big threat in slums they live.In rural areas language is vernacular,youths steal and do disturb peace among poor societies.
A good government is one that is ready to eradicate poverty through responsible means.

Governments in poor countries spend a lot of resource,money on different problems yet the root cause is poverty.You address issues of drug abuse,poor persons are consumers they want to relieve stress,spreading of contagious diseases,is related to poor person,they are bitter,sex is their main form entertainment as we shall see later.The problem is poverty in less developed country and that poverty is a parent of many children who keeps on bearing children.A poor person can invent a problem.

Communication of a poor person lacks respect in the way one speaks.The words of a poor person can oftenly lead to a confrontation.For them,understanding is a problem and therefore need someone who understands them.Their communication is demanding to impress good listeners.

As far as poor persons communication is concerned,their words shows great anger in them.A poor person is angry and not always happy when in self.A poor person is only happy in crowd but personally is not settled.One leads restless life.Most of them talk loud and think deep when alone.They do not care about their communication anymore.Modern poor people use advanced technologies to communicate such as facebook,twitter and the current networks to pass their angry information.It is only is poor societies where poor children claim to know more than their parents,youths more than elders,students more than their teachers.Follow their conversations and see.

It is because they are illiterate,ignorant,angry and bitter about their lives that is why their communication is poor both in the media and outside media.To reach persons,their communication is comedy and make the cores have fun.The communication of poor persons today is an investment that earns them money because of comedies in pronunciation of words.Some poor change their lives through such investment.

It is not important to forget this,a poor person likes hate speech,to hear words that have no respect for moral sake and if such speeches are likely to lead to conflict and in favour of them.That is how political leaders win elections among poor societies by throwing words that do not make sense for literacy purpose.Even as wars erupt,poor persons are in support of them not actually knowing that they,themselves are the one to suffer.The speech to call for or just to incite and ignite war and disunity is the good one for poor persons and in pure societies.

When poor persons communicate to their leaders they pretend and even use good names to please the rulers.They even compete to please their leaders so as to earn favour and small grands.Another aspect of poor man's speech is sexial practices centered,and food centric.A development speech is wanting in minds of poor persons.It takes long for a poor person to learn good communication practices.

Modern technology has reduced sounds,loud and noises that were produced by ancient poor to communicate.Today poor persons make noises on their phones calling their clients and listening,writing,reading,if they know,using their mobile phones for thosd who sacrifice to buy.Education is necessary for poor persons to learn good communication techniques.A poor person communicates to praise any rich person one knows.Furthermore,poor persons tend to waste their time speaking about politics.This makes them be idle and form groups to discuss political issues poorly and when it comes time for real politics,poor persons show their political poverty.

Poor persons are poor listeners and mostly do like to pretend to listen to what they are being told.They are poor listeners in the sense that they are lazy listeners,take-turn listeners,insecure listeners,self-centred and competitive listeners.Lazy listeners believe that listening involves no work and that they can just sit back and listen.Their attitude to listening is that listening is natural so they do not have to do anything.Unfortunately they find themselves at a lose for words if they are called upon to regurgitate the content of the listening text.They are take turn listeners because they do not want to listen to others but since they know they are expected to listen,they pretend to be listening when they are actually paying no attention.They only become interested when their turn to talk approaches but often communicates a prose appasses.The insecure listener is usually so worried about what is supposed to say for his audience and because they are concentrating on their own anxiety,insecure listeners do not notice what others are saying.

They are self centred listeners because they only listen for messages about themselves but if the message is about someone else they switch off.They are also competitive listeners because they regard listening as a competition that if you tell them about your plans to travel to Britain,they will tell you that they even have gone to both USA and Britain several times.It is the nature mostly of the relatively poor persons who can meet basic demands through their underemployment.The abjec poor will tell you many small things he has done in his life.The communication of relatively poor persons is full of arrogance and boastful.They talk in such away that absolute poor persons feel more and more inferior.Their communication shows their proud nature because of small privilege they have over others.Rich persons do have a good knowledge of communication skills.The problem is not themselves but their social status hence need to educate them communication skills in schools but it is not an easy task to change nature of their communication even if someone is taught.They have bitter kind of speech because of their pathetic rural and poor life.

Due to modern technology in which poor persons have no say,they are audiciously exploited by rich persons in terms of communication.The life of poor persons is also made difficult due to modern communication systems for instance use of mobile phones and simcards that have made communication more expensive in modern poor societies yet the poor persons embrace the move with anxiety and proud.The expenses incurred by poor persons in modern peripheries in terms of communications makes me realise that seemingly,the leaders among poor societies sold their poor citizens to rich persons who own technology of modern communications to exploit the poor masses as those rich persons gain a lot from the poor.This is because rich persons produce numbers technologically which they sell to the poor persons to earn money.Imagine somebody sets number you all know,produces them and in turn earn them money and ofcourse expensive.In most cases you will see poor persons praising improved communication services yet they are exploited.Modern expensive communication services will contribute to collapse of already collapsed poor persons.

A poor person talks using expensive mobile phones loudly and proudly without noting down how his or her little resources are being depleted.Modern technology in communication services is analogous to finding a very beautiful girl who does no job for you but you buy her,stay with her and maintain and the moment her beauty increases you pay more as she encourages you that you are her better chance.The girl advances everything from you yet you are still a poor person.The big problem with people in poor societies even if educated,with their education they cannot detect who and how they are exploited to the extent of no more exploitation but they are still exploited.Another big issue of concern is that such cores pay the few rich of poor socoeties to exploit and gain alot from the majority poor masses.To help save poor persons,good political leaders and emulators of good use of technology in their societies is required.

THE POOR AND POLITICS

A poor man is a poor political animal.You cannot separate poor persons from poor politics unless through thorough education on politics and other relevant fields which I also suspect may fail.Politics of tribe,clan,relatives,rich,corruption and self interest for money is inevitable among poor societies.They tend to be divided along ethinic lines by rich persons who will rule them forever.Problems in poor societies are not ethnic line based but are experienced by so long as you are poor.Poor persons are the sleeping lions of politics,rich will therefore always win and rule them more.

Poor persons during campaigns time to prepare for elections,they open their mouth and stomach wide during that short period of time,become good supporters of rich persons to overcome their hunger for food and money not forgetting they suffered for long instead they go to a position to choose poor leaders.Those poor leaders may both be rich or poor dependingly.

A poor person is not politically independent since their pplitical stand is determined by their superiors.Poor persons are political indecisive and when they decide,there is no rationale in their decisions.Since they are mostly illiterate,they are misled politically by those persons who want to gain from them.Even if poor persons pass through higher learning political education,it is difficult for them to change from poor politics.They are politically ignorant to extent that even when educated,it is not easy for them to change from politics of their villages,relatives,tribes,and societies.

During elections,poor persons vote for one of their own.They vote for relatives,their tribes people,those who gave them more money during campaigns and those who conducted expensive campaigns.Poverty is parallel to good politics.Poor persons vote to defend rich persons of their tribes or just societies.They really lack rationale in elections of their leaders.After election results is when poor persons minds open up and realise they chose bad leaders.In poor societies poor persons do not support their leaders yet they vote for them.This makes politics to become another economic activity of poor persons in poor societies even after campaign periods and elections.It is because poor persons realise they messed when voting,chose leaders without considering their benefits and demerits and therefore opposition gets more support from the poor persons after they have chosen the rulers who form the governments among developing countries.This makes politics in poor societies a continous activity.Development in such countries becomes a challenge because of harsh political environment between the governments and opposition sides since each part wants to defend its position.Wars and conflicts erupt in such societies because of poor politics.

It is only in poor countries where citizens claim opposition to have made good rulers and those who failed to have made good leaders.In most cases poor citizens do not support their governments any more.This makes such governments in poor countries to support their supporters and witness exploitation of poor persons.The supporters of governments in poor societies are rich persons and for that reason governments in poor countries work for the interest of the rich persons.Only the poor persons will cry in developing countries because of expenses in life.The few wise poor persons who support the rulers in poor societies gain favour and some eventually change their social status through government support.The government will only favour poor persons if they responsibly vote for good rulers to make the government and also if they support their goverment(those ruling).

The problem is that in developing societies,when campaigns come,poor citizens have forgotten how they have been suffering and still choose leaders they later do not support.Such ignorant behavior brings again rulers that poor chaps resist later on.In poor societies,governments are a cycle of unwanted leaders by their poor citizens.The irony is that poor persons voted for such governments.

My believe is that governments that exist in poor societies are good for such societies.They are the supposed leaders to rule those people.That is why poor persons are supposed to support their leaders they chose for development purposes.If they do not work together with their governments,unequal development will become the order of the day.Poor persons will oppose their leaders,think of overthrowing their governments but in vain since the nature of any government demands that government is stronger than any other entity of a state.All features of a state are in hands of government.Though government is an element of a state according to westphalian treaty of 1648,I know of government to be stronger than even the word state itself.I mean that revolution cannot help poor persons to overthrow modern governments among poor societies.

Today it is difficult to overthrow the governments as poor persons in poor countries alway think because of modern technologies owned by governments;communication,transport,military,and all others.People used to overthrow governments in past days because technologie were weak and even absent.I am very sure that if colonialism,European happened these modern days then our heroes and legends would not have made it to resist and struggle for our independence.Thanks for weak technology those days.Today it is difficult to overthrow the governmentd because of high technology owned by government.Modern coercive instruments are in the hands if government.The only type of revolution that can help poor persons is to revolve to elect leaders responsibly with highest rationale.Another one is to just give in and support the ruling governments if they fail to choose and even get good leaders and to wait for the right time of the same peacefully.

Ok,if it means to overthrow the government,which coersive instrument does the poor citizens own?Is there unity among poor citizens on political matters?If they try they are the one to suffer.The only group which I know to of having ability to overthrows its government is the military.Let us not try to reach their it is worse.If it happens,poor citizens will suffer and the only savior will be the hegemony(ies) like U.S.A if they realise the great loss of poor people and are willing to help.

Politics in poor societies are poor in the sense that,elections of leaders is poorly done.During voting,poor citizens are enticed with small amounts of money and other little material resources such as food to vote for their providing leaders.Rich persons influence poor with such bribes to vote for them.Since the only problem of the poor persons is to get instant money and food,it has become easy for poor leaders who have money to win in elections.A poor person cannot elect his or her fellow poor who have leadership skills and right intention to rule,rather they are denied chance to rule because they have no money to buy poor voters alcohol,food and give them other form of bribes.

Political leaders in poor societies have no right intention to lead.Such leaders have intention to get wealthier in leadership pisitions and will do what it takes them to get wealth when they rule.Right intention is to serve the people who elected you irregardless of social background.Right intetion to lead is fight for good of the people yet leaders in poor countries use their leadership power to satisify their self interests.It is true that those who lead among poor societies fight for their own self interests.Rationality for such leaders is poorly practised.They become corrupt and exploit poor citizens until no place to exploit but they persist exploitation.If their exists among them good leaders who want to serve for the good of all,one is threatened with death and losing of jobs.Such leaders work for personal development.

If they continue to lead that way,poor persons will tend to fight for their rights.They will think of revolutions.Since rulers are the government they will really impact to poor people using their coercive instruments such us police.I know poor persons cannot fight against governments and win or rather,they will lose their lives.

A good government,a good ruler if it means to lead its citizens,it must have right intention for its citizens irregardless of tribes,religion,and other social statuses.Government is charged with biggest responsibity for its citizens and therefore it must teach its affiliates good standards of leadership.It must not allow exploitation of its citizens by either means but right intention for all prevails among the governments of developed countries.

Corruption is key element among poor societies.Elections in poor societies are characterised by theft,rigging,deaths because of bribes in form of money needed by the facilitators of corruption.The problems is that poor persons are the ones used to practise bad politics.They are paid to kill others during elections by the candidates.Those poor youths are used to fight for candidates a matter which makes elections in poor societies to follow a conflictual nature.The political institutions are very weak and only serve for personal interests of their leaders.Election results in poor societies are featured with corruption,stealing.Election results takes no accountability and transparency.After elections when citizen meet they want where their elections went since they compare notes and found out they all vote for a person who was not announced the winner.Election institutions in developing countries are not trusted because their leaders work to maintain their status quo.

Democratically,poor societies are singers of democracy yet they are dancers of anti-democracy.Since in such societies poor persons are many and most of them illiterate,their leaders fight to steal in elections and some of them make the deal before even election dates are decided.That is why leaders rule for several years among poor societies without any change since institutions in such societies are weak and work for such rulers.It is habitual nature of leadership among poor societies.

In elections,those candidates who lack right intention to lead when their lose,their societal voters suffer.They are attacked by gangs who are paid by the losers to terorrise those poor voters.In elections,poor persons are the victims of any bad results of elections by the poor candidates.Such leaders do that for revenge of their bribes.Politics is another field where most of poor persons lose their lives.Since poor persons die almost in all occasions of life,others in politics,crimes,etc,there number continues to reduce and they will still lose their lives more for rich person to live well.It therefore calls for the wellwishers to eradicate poverty so as to save lives for the poor.Poverty calls for pathetic life situations and eventually deaths of poor persons.

Poor persons are not politically independent.Their political actions are directed by the rich persons who want to gain a lot from them.During election times is when rich persons can allow poor persons in their homes,is when they can chat and laugh altogether and share meals.A poor person is used as a machine and a tool to make leaders attain positions in political field.They are driven,moved by those who take opportunity of their pathetic life and divide them along tribal,clan gender,party,religion and social,education and economic lines and continue to lead them as poor persons maintain their gradges over each line,war and fight along such lines.It is because poor persons are easily swayed to believe.

Modern poor persons cannot overthrow rich people from power in modern world because of disunity among poor persons in poor societies.Modern poor persons speak different languages.Their communication is poor and do not work together as their heroes and heroines and legends did do to sent home colonialists.Modern people should not therefore risk to turn against the core in their government.Democracy brought poor persons a right chance to responsibly vote and elect good leaders.Electioneering is the right revolution to do by participating responsibly.Problem comes where election riggings arise something which makes poor persons more agitated.They get lacrity to undertake revolution but the problem is that poor persons fight against each other based on tribal and groups lines.Each group fights for their rich persons to rule until the best warring group leads.It is very bad to steal in elections because it the greatest since a person can commit in this world because more life is lost through wars and conflicts.

Another nature of politics of poor persons is that this peripherals in less developed countries,peripheries,are not allowed by their leaders who are cores to unite instead leaders and ruling class divide them in different groups,tribes,clans so as they continue warring and conflicting along group lines as they are ruled.That is why poor persons their are politically enemies.If their exists somebody to unite poor persons,his her life is endangered and eventually one is killed and dies through a mystery way.Good leaders who want to rule for the good of their people are endangered species among poor societies.They die of the actions by the cores on them through terrible and unbelievable means.

For that reason,poor persons continue to have political differences that leads for their constant wars and conflicts against each other for political power among perpherals.In such societies to win in elections one has to incite his or her society against others and talk evil of their enemies.Even candidates do the same against their competitors.The more you make the poor happy the more your chances to win through telling evil of your competitors and enemies.That is how poor politics is practised by poor persons where they are divided along family,clan,social,economical and tribes lines to be ruled.When such rulers win they lead for their personal development yet the poor voters are left in disagreements that make them war and fight against each other such that when they come again to seek votes they win using the same procedure.The truth is that poverty in any place does not consider family,clan,tribe.You can not say that richest people come in my tribe yet you are poor as the poor persons do in poor societies.The richman knows that the time poor persons unite,he will be overthrown from power and therefore the core cannot allow the peripherals to unite.Politically,modern poor persons are not united.Politics of hatred and incitement is rampant in poor countries.

Political leaders among poor societies do fight for their self interests to enrich themselves yet do little to develop their societies.That is why most casea you will hear that among the cores of the world,some of them come from very poor societies.So you wonder in lacrity what really happens in poor societies.When I was in High school my teacher used to ask if it is prudent for top student to score a hundred percent marks while the rest scored below average by far.We reached a conclusion that the top student is abnormal or does unique things others do not know.The rest of the class was graded to be normal since it seemed out that the rest shared and learned to help each other.So you can apply that to leadership among poor societies that there is abnormal leadership where very few are rich and the rest very poor.What can change the lives of poor persons is politics and technology.Politics in the sense that poor persons need to choose able leaders who will serve for their full good since politics is everything in all aspects of human life.That they are political leaders who determine everything in a society is the reason.Technology comes in to enhance,facilitate and amplify creation of wealth.

Since poor persons are disciples and followers of poor politics,their status quo is not likely to change unless they embrace and conform to the norms of good politics.Participating responsiponsibly and with right intention and being rational in political activiities that people undertake are the necessary requirements and foundations,basics of good politics.

Political apathy is the nature of poor persons in developing countries.They do not know about their political leaders,political rights of their countries,benefits of chosing leaders responsibly and responsible ones and therefore end up voting for poor leaders who bribed them in elections period.Poor persons are ignorant about their political environment yet they suffered alot from poor leaders they chosen.Such peripheral people do not know the nature of political status in their societies and are ignorant of political leadership.Democracy helps them chance to elect good leadership yet they take it for granted.Their eyes,minds and ears open after they have irresponsibly and ignorantly elected for unsupposed leaders due to their illiteracy.Something about poor persons is that even if you educate them about pure and clean politics,they are likely not to change but to shame you through their actions.

It is only in poor societies where politics is viewed as a dirty game.Politics of hatred,murder,rape and theft,of our own,our tribe,our son and our daughter.A poor person can not defent democracy since they are bribed to disregard.This is because a poor person lacks money,one is very hungry and is driven by such immediate demands.This makes poor persons politically weak and wiked.Modern poor persons are seemingly to have realised the essence of good politics but still are driven by poverty to disarm strengths of democracy.It is for that reason that I confirm,democratization will not achieve its objectives in presence of poverty,never.It demands for supporters of democracy if they are governments,multinational corporations,both states and non-states actors to help eradicate poverty.They will find it easy to overcome poverty if poor persons in peripheral states elect good and right intentions oriented leaders who does not involve in corrupt activities in whatsoever means.It will happen if the institutions that exists in poor societies get stronger to fight for poor persons rights and not for interests of the bosses and other political leaders for instance leaders of poll bodies in such societies should learn the essence of pure and not poor politics,democracy oriented.The problem is that poor societies are democratic yet they are led by dictators.

THE POOR AND ENTERTAINMENT

Enternainment is vanguard activity of poor persons to make happy their rich rulers.Infact modern poor persons in modern poor societies tend to entertain their political leaders through songs,dances and other cultural and traditional frenzies.I have seen many poor persons who earn their income through entertaining leaders in different occasions as we shall see later in this topic.

Sexual intercourse is the main form of entertainment among poor persons and in poor societies.The peripheries of the peripheries tend to enjoy sexual practices most of their times due to idlesness and last.That is the reason,among others,why poor persons give birth to many children since sex is their only business and activity they enjoy doing through their hardwork as compared to difficult tasks they toil and moil to accomplish in their lives as a sources of their incomes.Following that observation,poor persons hold their discussions more oftenly on sexual matters;who is good or bad man and woman for sexual engagements,how you can do it better and best.The vocabulary especially vernacular kind that poor adults and their children is that of bedroom affairs in particular sexual intercourse.The practice is what poor persons claim that they share with rich persons.

Poor children start engaging in sexual matters onces they realise they are okay to go.Poor children in modern poor societies already have their babies,their sexual diseases and their own husbands and wives.In most cases those families of children do rely on the parents for survival especially fathers's parents albeit modern type try also to get help from mothers's families.It is because poor persons are sex oriented;you find men talking about women and women do the same about men and that is the nature of their discussions.It is among poor families you will mostly hear that certain man is sexually weak,and his wife announces that in public.Elders in poor societies today solve sexually related issues for different poor couples since the only issues they see touchy in family is that.Poor societies value sex alot than any other thing on earth and ofcourse poor persons think of getting money to enjoy sex with beautiful

ladies they admire whatever the case,married or not.A poor person loves the intercourse a lot to extent that they refer to process as eating and the parts that do sex as food.Eating is another lovely activity for them and that is why sex is
is sometimes reffered to as food by poor persons.

Due to value of sex among poor persons,men keep on hunting beautiful girl,boys do the same for girls.Their minds are sex centric to the level that development is not a bother in their life.Poor youths waste their times in boy girl relationships,boys searching for girls always.Poor persons prefer food to sex because,sex is only enjoyous games in their minds.A poor man can not live without wive(s) as per his traditions or else the society will punish him especially through gossips.The first thing a poor man thinks of is how he will get wife and marry and minds of poor women is how to secure their husbands.It is difficult to avoid this in their minds with solemn main reason of bring frequent sexual intercourse very close and particularly a poor man wants frequent sex.The big punishment poor women do for their poor husbands is to deny them sexual service.A poor woman respects a poor man because of how poor man does the activity.Poor persons claim that wives do not respect their husbands solemnly because of inadequate sexual satisfaction and it works very well among them.Poor men claim that the only think that can keep wives home is serious sexual intercourse.

Since poor persons are many and do play big role in political voting and to help other businesses grow as they customers,many politicians win the minds of poor persons through discussing with them bedroom matters as they had read minds of many poor persons.Communications stations do consider a lot on bedroom issue to secure large numbers of customers in modern world since that is where poor persons can contribute a lot and become happy about.Many churches that have emerged among poor societies do exist because they do the same to find more clients.From their you can learn a lot why churches do not serve their roles in modern poor socueties.

Considering the above observations,modern world is full of difficulties of life.Modern poor girls are taught against premature sex yet few of them do heed.The nature of modern world is that what was earlier in deficit is now becoming plenty and vise versa,what was supported earlier by few is becoming to be supported by many and its opposite;things change to occupy the positions that were originally occupied by their opponents.Modern girls have learnt it not to subject themselves into early sexual matters.Modern poor boy do pass through difficulties to quench their sexual thirsts and what most of them opt to do is to start raping younger and older girls in their presence if some cannot agree with other poor girls who depict sex as their main form of entertainment.Others enter into other sexual malpractices.And because modern poor girls do not like poor boys,such poor boys still enter into rapist gangs to cause defilements to girls.But since rich persons marry beautiful girls from poor families and societies,the problem arises from sexual intercourse since a rich man does not value sex such a lot in his life that every often is engaging in sex with his wife instead one things of his development concerns.Such situations make wives of those rich persons to seek sexual service from the poor men they know.This gives another nature of poor societies that adultery,rape and other forms of sexual malpractices are rampant.

The modern world poor persons are forced to be creative in order to survive.Despite the fact that life is not easy for modern poor persons,they have resolved to commercialise sex in particular poor women because they have realised men in such poor societies love sex and they will have to buy from them to enjoy the activity.That is how most of modern poor women earn to sustain their lives.The worst comes when such women are employed,they sell their bodies for sex in favour of promotion,job security and other things they want.Infact modern poor women have made work places and offices to be prostitution centres since minds of men in poor societies are very weak and vulnerable to sexual likenableness.It is such pathetic situation in poor socities such that to attack prostitution,rape and other sexual malpractices,poverty is the elephant in the house.And most important thing in poor societies today is that people do involve in sexual dalliance,very illicit and that forms joyous part of their entertainment.Persons in poor societies are sexual sentiments.Couples elusively practise illict sexual practices outside marriagesThat is why I damn persons in poor societies as sexual immorals.

Following that persons in poor societies are sexual animals,their marriage is devoid of trustworthiness and faithfulness.Today poor couples do not trust each other because they do love sex a lot something that makes them try to explore intercourses with different people as that is the only development issue of their minds concern.A have not husbands and wives in modern world do not know the actual number of people they have slept with;they are many and also modern poor boys and girls.The future marriages for modern have nots youths is fool of troubles since sexual matters have messed modern youths through early enjoyement of sex,there are no virgins to marry.Infact poor persons are always depressed and obessed in relationship for sex purposes and that makes them own lust for sexual intercourse.It is from the lust for sex that makes poor persons spread and contract contagious and viral diseases.

Another form of entertainment among peripheries in peripherals are singing and dancing in coordination with drinking traditional and other liquors.They sing and dance to entertain political leaders.Others through comedies do the same to appease their leaders.The main interesting part of it is that they keep in fields playing their talents while the lords of wealth manage the offices and their taxes.Poor persons in poor countries are heavily taxed both directly or indirectly.Their leaders tend to fool them with free things that requires their large contribution so that they do not know what is really happening on the ground.

Also important is that food makes poor persons happy.Hunger makes one very angry.Food entertains poor persons and they do say that friendship is in stomach in addition to relationship.The problem is that poor persons lack balanced diet and as a result do feed on alot amount of their staple food to kill hunger.

THE POOR AND EDUCATION

Absolutely poor persons consider education as a corrupt activity that favours rich persons on earth.Others think the meaning of education is to study foreign language,is a colonial activity and so means nothing in life.That education is not everything is their stand.The amazing part of it is that a child of a poor person is an academic genius if education only meant academic performance.

Education of peripherals in modern societies is seen to have gained success in terms of its name education.This is because today the question of quality and standard is lacking among the poor.For rich,education is standard in developed countries and that is why the children of the cores of a periphery do not study in those peripheries instead they attain education in core states.The same rich children comes back to handle all the operations of a periphery.Ask where the son or daughter of a rich person studied,the answer is outside your poor country.Let me complete it,in a core state.

Poor children though clever,they lack financial,material and environmental support to win poverty.Today all poor in modern societies love education.You will meet many schools everywhere you step in poor societies and a large sum of them just a mere buildings.Universities are many in poor societies because of commercial education activities since there are many poor persons who will become their clients in such peripheries.Education today will become useless since no standard measure,no quality matters raised in poor countries.

The poor persons are always on roads early in the morning and evening going to school day in day out.It has become their prestigious activity since if you asked one will claim am a student.Almost everybody you meet in poor societies is a student but their actions are different from that of a student yet they truely school.

Poor children suffer a lot of challenges in education because they have no say in life.Rich children rig to be given certificates,diplomas,degrees masters etc even if they have not schooled.A poor person struggles with book.A poor child will rely on long procedures and legals of government that a rich person wont tolerate.The rest are history.